THE AMAZING STARDUST FRIENDS

STEP INTO THE SPOTLIGHT!

By Heather Alexander

Illustrated by Diane Le Feyer

BRANCHES™

SCHOLASTIC INC.

READ ALL ABOUT

THE AMAZING STARDUST FRIENDS

☆ Table of Contents ☆

For my sparkly niece, Marlo — H.A.

To my sweet, sweet darling Gaïa — D.L.

Library of Congress Cataloging-in-Publication Data

Alexander, Heather, 1967-
Step into the spotlight! / by Heather Alexander ; illustrated by Diane Le Feyer.
pages cm. — (The Amazing Stardust Friends ; [1])
Summary: Bella, Carly, and Allie live and work at the Stardust Circus, and when Marlo arrives, eager to make friends and become part of the show, she tries aerial arts, juggling, and even dog training as she tries to find her own special talent, with lots of help from the other girls.
ISBN 0-545-75752-5 (pbk.) — ISBN 0-545-75753-3 (hardcover) — ISBN 0-545-76090-9 (ebook) [1. Circus—Fiction. 2. Ability—Fiction. 3. Friendship—Fiction.] I. Le Feyer, Diane, illustrator. II. Title.
PZ7.A37717Bri 2015
[Fic]—dc23
2014017063
ISBN-13: 978-93-5103-841-2

Illustrated by Diane Le Feyer
Book design by David DeWitt
Edited by Katie Carella

First Scholastic printing, January 2015
Reprinted by Scholastic India Pvt. Ltd., April., June 2015, 2018

Printed at Shivam Offset Press, New Delhi.

1 Big, Sparkly Dream

"Look! That girl is flying!" I cried.

She soared over my head. Her shiny blue leotard sparkled in the spotlight. Her dark hair was pulled into a glittery bun.

She was up so high. Almost at the ceiling!

Loud music filled the big tent. I bounced to the beat.

My mom sat next to me. She looked up at the flying girl, too. "I love the trapeze, Marlo!" she shouted over the music. "It's my favorite part of the circus!"

I had waited for weeks and weeks to see the circus. And I had waited for weeks and weeks for what was going to happen *after* tonight's show.

That's when I was starting a new life.

A whole new, sparkly, *amazing* life for me—Marlo Sophia Sommer!

I was joining the famous Stardust Circus! For real!

Living with the circus would be exciting, and a little scary.

I took a huge bite of my pink cotton candy. I let it melt on my tongue.

"Ladies and gentlemen!" Liam the Ringmaster called into a microphone. His job was to introduce each act. He wore a red silk top hat and a red vest. Liam gave my mom her new job at the circus.

"Are you ready for BIG fun?" Liam called to the crowd.

"Yes!" everyone cried.

"Then put your hands together for the last act in tonight's show. The fabulous Stardust Circus parade!" Liam called.

The crowd clapped and cheered.

"Whoo-hoo!" I stomped my feet.

A girl my age galloped in on a snowy-white horse. The horse's mane and tail were braided with pink and purple ribbons. The girl had ribbons in her superlong hair, too.

The girl stood up on the horse's back.

While the horse was moving!

Then she flipped into a backbend.

And she stayed like that—on top of the *moving* horse!

"Do you see *her*?" I grabbed Mom's arm and pointed. "And *her*?"

A girl clown in a pink satin dress and striped tights danced around. She had hot-pink braids and fake butterflies around her head. Pink glitter covered her freckles. A pink star was painted on the tip of her nose. She looked eight years old, just like me.

She smiled and waved to the crowd.

I waved back.

Then that trapeze girl did so many back handsprings that I lost count.

Next, the girl with the superlong hair jumped off her horse. She held hands with the clown girl and the trapeze girl.

"Meet the Stardust Girls!" called Liam.

The three girls danced and led the parade.

Suddenly, I wanted to wear a sparkly outfit. I wanted to dance and flip and fly and make people laugh. I wanted to be friends with these glittery girls. And, more than anything, I wanted to be in the big circus parade!

2 Home, Sweet Train

The parade finished. The circus was over.

Liam the Ringmaster met up with Mom and me. We walked down many streets. I had a fluttery, scared feeling in my belly.

I'd always lived in our same house. I'd always had the same friends. Until now.

"Our Great Adventure is starting," Mom whispered. "You and me. M and M."

M and M is what we call ourselves. For Marlo and Mom. My dad left when I was a bitty baby. I really don't feel sad about it anymore, because Mom and I are super-close. We always stick together. We look alike, too—blonde hair, green eyes, and pointy nose and chin.

We stopped at the train tracks. I twisted my neck, trying to find the end to the longest train I had ever seen. The train was painted *purple* with STARDUST CIRCUS in big gold letters along the side.

"I read that each part of a train is called a *car*," I told Liam. "And everyone from the circus lives here. Even all the horses and dogs!"

"You know your stuff." Liam stepped up. "Climb aboard!"

My belly stopped fluttering. We were going to live on a train! No one in my old town lived on a train.

We walked through the train and stopped at a gold door.

"Welcome to your awesome new home!" said Liam.

I liked how Liam said things were *amazing* and *awesome* and *fabulous.*

Our door had a doorbell—just like in a real apartment.

I buzzed it a few times. Then a few more.

We stepped inside.

THE STARDUST CIRCUS TRAIN!

MEDIA & GAME CAR
HORSES
Bella's Family
CIRCUS OFFICE
SAFE
PERFORMERS' APARTMENTS
DRESSING ROOM CAR
PIE CAR
Marlo & Mom
LOCOMOTIVE ENGINE
PROPS CAR
CREW & STAFF
ACTING CAR

3 The Pie Car

"Wow! It's quite cozy," Mom said, looking around.

I knew that meant Mom thought it was small. But it was perfect. Our new home had a mini-kitchen, a bathroom, and bunk beds for me and Mom.

"I call the top bunk!" I yelled. It would be fun to share with Mom.

The boxes we'd packed were stacked in a corner. Next to the boxes stood my hula-hoops. I *love* to hula-hoop.

"Now, where will these fit?" Mom asked, picking one up.

I looked around. Then I had an idea. "Why don't we hang them on the wall—like art?"

"Perfect!" Mom likes my crafty ideas.

The train let out a loud whistle. I grabbed on to a stool as the train began to move.

"We're off to the town of Scarlet for our next show," said Liam. "Are you hungry? After a show, the performers all head to the Pie Car for food."

"Let's go!" I wasn't hungry, but I was curious about the Pie Car.

When my mom first told me about it, I had pictured a car filled with apple and cherry pies.

But the Pie Car is the name of the restaurant on the circus train. My mom used to be the chef at De-Lish, a restaurant in our old town. Her French toast with powdered sugar was famous. (The mountains of powdered sugar were my idea!) But De-Lish closed.

So Mom had said it was time for something exciting and a little bit scary. And she joined the circus as a chef!

Liam led us inside the Pie Car. It was right next door to our apartment. The walls were painted pale olive green. Booths lined both walls. The tabletops were old and chipped.

“Yuck!” I said.

“Shhh,” warned Mom. But I knew she didn’t like it, either. The Pie Car was *not* pretty.

Liam nodded. “Marlo is right. It needs work.”

“Hey, I can fix up the Pie Car,” I said.

Mom smiled as I began making a list.

Hummmmmmm. I heard a noise.

Then I heard the tooting of a trumpet.

And the crash of a cymbal.

The door opened, and I gasped.

4 The Stardust Girls!

Men and women tooting trumpets and banging drums entered the Pie Car. I had seen them in the parade.

The brass players and drummers sat on swivel stools at the tall counter. Mom's kitchen was on the other side of the counter. The tuba player found a small booth. His tuba sat across from him.

Would the Stardust Girls be coming, too?

I chewed my thumbnail nervously. Back home, I had been best friends with Kira. We both loved strawberry ice cream and hated mushrooms. But I didn't really know anything about the Stardust Girls.

Would they like me? Would I like them? I hoped so.

I heard laughing. The clowns came in. Happy clowns. Funny clowns.

And then I saw her. The girl clown with the pink braids!

She rushed over to me. "Hi! You're the new girl, aren't you? I'm Carly Bruni."

"Yes, I'm Marlo," I said. "You were great in the parade. You made me laugh."

Carly's blue eyes twinkled. "I love making people laugh." She turned. "Oh, good! Allie's here."

The trapeze girl walked in on her hands!

Totally upside down.

She stopped next to me and stayed upside down. "I'm Alejandra Padillo Falto. My friends call me Allie. I'm eight."

"Hi! I'm Marlo." I had never talked to anyone who was upside down before. She turned right side up.

Then the girl who rode the horse skipped over. Little jewels shone in the shape of a heart on her cheek.

"And here's Bella Lu!" Carly hugged her. Carly had lots of pep. That's what my mom calls it when I'm bursting with energy.

Bella held something furry in her hands.

"What's that?" I asked.

"Boris the guinea pig," she said softly. "I'm teaching him to ring a bell and play a song."

"Bella is crazy for animals," said Carly. "She taught ballet to the dogs."

"Dogs can dance?" I asked. Boris sniffed my hand.

"Sure they can," said Allie. "Didn't they have dancing dogs in your old circus?"

"My *old* circus?" I said. "I've never been in a circus."

Allie tilted her head. "If you're not a circus person, why are you here?"

I chewed my nail again. Then I pointed into the kitchen. "My mom is the new cook. I'll help sometimes, too. I bake yummy brownies."

"I *so* wish I could cook," said Carly.

"I could teach you," I said. "And I have a great plan to make over this Pie Car. We can do it together, okay?"

"Oh, that would be fun!" Bella smiled.

"Marlo!" Mom waved me over.

"I have to go," I said.

"See you in school tomorrow," said Carly.

School? On a circus train?

5 Let's Make a Deal

The next morning, I picked at my toast with strawberry jelly.

"Ready for school, Marlo?" Mom asked.

"I don't think I'm going to like it. Kira won't be there." I had always gone to school with Kira. I wouldn't know anyone at this new school.

"Moving is hard. But remember, it's a Great Adventure, too." Mom smoothed my bangs. "What about those girls you met yesterday?"

I pressed my nose against the window. The train rumbled on the tracks. Green fields whizzed by. And a cow! "Those girls all do *amazing* things."

"You do amazing things, too. You bake. You're crafty," she said.

I shook my head. Mom didn't get it. "I want to do amazing *circus* things, Mom. I want to be in the parade with those girls."

"You'll need to ask Liam about that," she said. "And maybe you will learn circus things in school."

"Will I learn to walk on my hands? That would be so much better than math."

Mom put her arm around me. "Let's go find out."

Mom and I walked down the narrow halls.

"There's Liam!" I rushed over to him. His top hat nearly touched the train's ceiling. "Liam, can I be in the circus parade?"

He raised his thick eyebrows. "Well, you will need to show me something fabulous."

"Fabulous?" I asked.

"Yes! Amazing and awesome, too. If you do, you're in. Deal?" He put out his hand.

"Deal." I shook Liam's hand. Mom smiled.

As we walked to school, I added up the days: Today we were on the train. Tomorrow afternoon we would stop to set up. Then the next day was the show.

That gave me only two days.

Could I find something fabulous, amazing, and awesome to do in only *two* days?

"We're here," Mom said. She pushed open a door that said SCHOOL CAR.

6 Crazy Circus School

The long car looked like a classroom. Desks lined each wall. A teacher's desk sat up front. There was a whiteboard and many windows.

Outside, farms rushed by.

Inside, a mini-circus was going on!

"Hi, Marlo!" Carly zoomed about on a unicycle. Two boys chased her. How did she balance on *one* wheel?

Bella sat at a desk. She held three ribbon leashes. At the end of each ribbon, a white dog in a tutu and a pearl necklace lifted a paw.

"Marlo, meet Coconut, Marshmallow, and Tofu," said Bella.

"Wow!" I said. "In my old school, we just had one fat hamster inside a cage."

Allie and two older girls sprawled on the floor. Allie was reading a book—with her feet wrapped around her head!

I gave her a small wave. She didn't wave back. *Maybe she didn't see me?* I thought.

A young woman hurried over to Mom and me. "Welcome, Marlo. I am Miss Ross," she said. She wore regular teacher clothes, cherry-red glasses, and bright red lipstick.

Then Miss Ross went *clap-snap-clap* with her hands. Everyone quickly sat down. I sat next to Carly. Mom waved good-bye.

As Miss Ross took attendance, I listened closely to see how everyone fit together. Danna and Renata were Allie's big sisters. They had the same honey-brown skin and dark curly hair as Allie. Carly's little brother, Leo, was there. So was Bella's big brother, Shen.

This taking-attendance part felt like regular school—especially when Miss Ross passed out math worksheets.

"Miss Ross! Miss Ross!" Carly raised her hand. "I have a present for you." She held out a sunflower.

Leo groaned. "Not again."

"How sweet!" Miss Ross leaned forward and took a big sniff.

A huge spurt of water shot out from the sunflower!

It splattered Miss Ross's glasses!

Uh-oh! Carly was going to get into *big* trouble.

But Miss Ross just laughed. "What a funny trick flower!"

She reached into her pocket. She tried to pull out a cloth to wipe her glasses. It was stuck.

"Marlo, would you help me?" she asked.

I hurried over. I gave the white square a tug.

"Whoa!" I cried. A blue square was attached to the white square.

I gave another tug. A bright green square was attached to the blue square. Then yellow. Then red.

I pulled and pulled. The chain of colorful squares grew longer and longer.

I laughed. "How does all that fit into your tiny pocket?" I asked.

"It's a clown trick," Miss Ross said. "I'm a clown, just like Carly."

My teacher is a clown? I thought.

Miss Ross was *not* a regular teacher. And this was *not* a regular school.

I couldn't wait to see what came next!

7 Lunch Bunch

For a clown, Miss Ross had us do an awful lot of not-funny schoolwork that morning.

"Time for lunch," she said. "And then dance class after that."

Finally! I was starving!

Carly turned to me. "Eat with us?"

"Sure!" I blurted out. Carly was so nice. And I couldn't wait to tell Kira that I was becoming friends with a clown.

I grabbed my books and followed Carly, Bella, and Allie to the Pie Car.

We all had grilled cheese.

Carly took a big bite. "Yum! It's extra cheesy."

"Your mom is a good cook," said Bella.

"Thanks," I said. Then I told them about my deal with Liam. "I really, really want to be in the circus parade. But Liam said I have to show him something fabulous that I can do."

"Can you ride a unicycle?" asked Carly.

I shook my head.

"Can you do backflips on a trampoline?" asked Allie.

I shook my head.

"Can you do a cartwheel on a dancing horse?" asked Bella.

I shook my head. "I've never tried riding a unicycle. I've never done a backflip. I've never even ridden a *non*-dancing horse."

"Well, that's a problem," Allie said, pulling the crusts off her grilled cheese.

"Oh, come on." Carly kicked Allie under the table. "Don't listen to her, Marlo. If you've never tried, how do you know you can't do amazing things?"

That got me thinking. Maybe I *could* fly through the air or stand on a horse.

"Can you guys help me find something special to do?" I asked.

"Yes!" agreed Carly.

"Well—" Allie began.

"We'll help you," Bella said, standing up. "But first, we have dance class. We're late!"

"I'm not done eating," I said.

Carly popped the rest of my grilled cheese into her mouth. Her cheeks bulged as she chewed. "Now you are!"

I laughed. "Let's go, then!"

8 Let's Dance!

My feet felt cold on the wood floors of the Dance Car. I watched Allie, Carly, and Bella in the tall mirrors.

They all wore pretty leotards. I wore leggings and a tank top.

"Marlo, we are working on the parade dance today," said Nia, our dance teacher.

"She doesn't need to know our dance," said Allie.

I looked at my feet. She was right. I wasn't in the parade . . . not yet anyway.

"She can try it, Allie," said Bella.

"Totally," agreed Carly.

Nia showed me the dance steps. *Kick, kick, kick, sway, arms up, twirl.*

The other girls kicked their legs high.

I kicked my legs not-so-high.

"Keep trying," called Carly.

I kicked. I swayed. And then . . .

"What comes next?" I asked.

"Arms." Bella showed me.

"Again," said Nia.

"Oops!" I said. "I forgot how to start."

"It's easy." Allie rolled her eyes. "Start with a high kick."

My cheeks burned. I was trying *really* hard.

I kicked. I swayed. I put my arms up. But I kept looking over at Allie. I could tell that she didn't want me there.

I *had* to show her that I could do the dance. I twirled around and around.

Whoa! I couldn't stop twirling. The Dance Car was spinning. I felt dizzy.

Bella laughed. "You're funny, Marlo!"

Allie laughed, too, but in a not-so-nice way.

I looked away.

"I have an idea, Marlo!" Carly cried. "You can be a *clown* in the parade! I'll show you how to be a *fabulous* clown!"

9 Who Are You?

After class, Carly and I raced through the train. Carly's legs were superlong. I tried my best to keep up.

"Is your hair really pink?" I asked. Her hair was still in two bright pink braids.

"My mom lets me put in wash-out color. It's called Party Pink. I mean, who ever heard of a clown with brown hair?" Her words came out as fast as she moved. "But don't tell anyone it's not really-truly pink, okay?"

"Promise," I said.

"I am a pink clown with pretty pink hair!" Carly twirled in the hall. "Who are you?"

What a strange question! "I'm Marlo."

"No, silly!" Carly giggled. She giggled a lot. "What kind of a clown are you? Every clown needs a *Look*. That's why I've brought you to the Wardrobe Car."

Carly pushed open a door.

Racks and racks of fabulous costumes filled the room. My eyes took in the bright colors, feathers, and sequins. There were tall hats and sparkly tiaras, too.

"I want to look funny and fancy," I said.

Carly pulled out a long black-velvet gown. "This dress is fancy."

I shook my head. "But it's not funny. I like a *lot* of colors."

"Carly?" called a voice.

"That's my mom." Carly put the gown back. Then we poked our heads through a rack of feathered boas.

"Hello there," Carly's mom said. She pinned lavender fabric onto a dress form. "You must be Marlo."

"Hi, Mrs. Bruni," I said. Then I pointed to the fabric. "What are you doing?"

"I'm making a dance costume," she said. "I'm the costume designer. I make everyone's sparkly outfits."

I looked at the fabric in a puddle at her feet. Suddenly, I had one of my great ideas!

I told Carly's mom all about the Pie Car makeover. "This lavender fabric would make amazing tablecloths!" I spotted purple ribbon nearby. "And they can be trimmed with ribbon!" I added.

"Love, love, love!" Carly's mom had as much pep as Carly. "I can sew them for you later."

"Thank you," I said.

“Now, let’s find your Clown Look, Marlo!” Carly tugged me away. “Dress or pants? Stripes or polka dots? Plain or pattern?” We zigzagged through the racks. She tossed skirts, long gloves, and hats into my arms.

“The fun part about being a clown is that nothing has to match,” Carly said. “Wear what you love.”

Soon I found my Clown Look.

“Ta-da!” I cried. “Check me out!”

10 Rainbow Fairy Clown

"I am a Rainbow Fairy Clown," I told Mom, Allie, Bella, and Carly.

I showed off my new outfit in the Pie Car before dinner.

Rainbow tutu. Rainbow-striped tights. And a teeny-tiny sequined top hat.

“I love it,” Mom said. “But where’s the fairy part?”

“There are fairy wings. I may or may not wear them,” I said. “But with wings, I could be a flying clown. I’ll be funny.”

“Clowns do more than be funny,” said Carly. “I ride a unicycle. Leo does magic. We both juggle.”

Carly reached into one of her many pockets. She kept a lot of clown stuff in her pockets. She pulled out three scarves. Pink, purple, and red.

Up in the air went one . . . two . . . three scarves. She caught one. Then she tossed it again to catch the next. She juggled fast. The colors became a beautiful blur.

We all cheered. Then Mom pointed to a carton of eggs on the counter. "Marlo, will you help me make egg salad?"

"Sure." I turned to Carly, Bella, and Allie. "I am great at peeling and chopping eggs. I chop them really tiny. That's what makes Mom's egg salad taste so good. I'll show you how."

"Hello, hello!" called Liam in his deep voice. He entered the kitchen.

This was my chance to show Liam what a fabulous clown I could be!

I grabbed three eggs. Juggling those would be fabulous.

"Marlo, those eggs aren't—" Mom began. I heard Mom, but I sent the eggs high into the air.

One . . . two . . . three . . .

I tried to catch them.

Splat!

Splat!

Splat!

"—cooked," finished Mom.

"Oh, no!" I cried.

Liam was covered with drippy, yellow yolk!

Carly giggled. Bella and Allie stared.

"I tried to tell you, Marlo," Mom said. She wiped Liam's shirt with a dish towel.

My face grew hot. "Sorry, Liam."

Liam didn't seem angry. Just very yolky.

"You need more practice, Marlo. Juggle one. Then move onto two," he said.

"But I don't have time to practice. The show is in two days. Maybe I can be the funny clown who *can't* juggle?" I said hopefully.

"Nope," said Liam. "Can you do any other circus things?"

I gulped. Carly looked at me and shrugged.

Then she looked over at Allie. Allie didn't say anything, so Carly spoke up. "How about aerial arts?"

"What are aerial arts?" I whispered to Bella.

"*Aerial* means up in the air," she whispered. "It's acrobatics in the sky."

"Great idea," said Liam. "Marlo can practice with Allie tomorrow."

Allie frowned. "Marlo won't be able to—"

Carly elbowed her. "Give her a chance," she whispered.

Allie shrugged. "Sure."

I could tell Allie didn't think I could be a Stardust Girl.

But I wanted it more than anything.

I'll show both Liam and Allie that I belong in the parade, I decided. *Tomorrow, I will learn to fly!*

11 Flip, Flop

On Saturday afternoon, the train finally stopped moving. We had made it to Scarlet. The crew people started setting up the big tent for tomorrow's show. The train's ceilings were too low to practice aerial arts. So we had to walk to a gym in the town to practice.

Allie's parents, sisters, and cousins led the way. I followed with Allie. Her family had once been aerialists in Mexico. They called themselves the Flying Faltos.

"Chocolate, molinillo, corre, corre que te pillo!" They sang a Spanish song loudly.

Allie was the loudest.

My belly flip-flopped. I hoped I could do aerial arts. I didn't want Allie to laugh at me again.

When we got to the gym, the Flying Faltos stretched. I stretched, too.

I touched my toes.

I tried a split. *Ouch!*

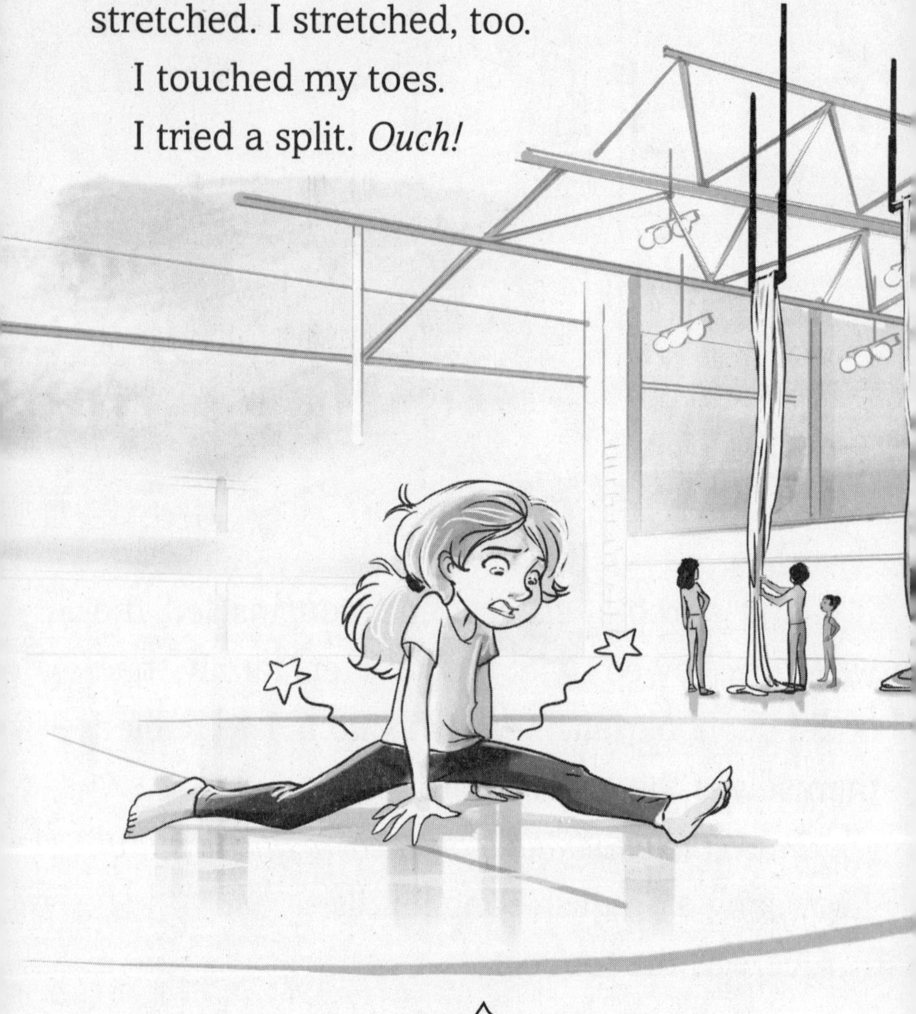

“What are those long, hanging pieces of fabric?” I asked, pointing to the ceiling. “They look like fancy living room curtains.”

“They’re called *silks*,” said Allie.

Then Allie’s sister Danna climbed the silks using only her arms. High above the floor, she twisted the silks around one foot. She flipped upside down. She bent her back and pointed her toes. Danna looked so graceful!

Allie jumped up and grabbed onto the fixed trapeze bar. She somersaulted over it. Then she held onto the bar with only the tops of her feet!

Allie was short. But she was strong.

"I can stay upside down forever," she said, showing off. "I have superstrong feet."

I wiggled my own feet. They looked too weak to hold a pencil!

"I think I'll try the silks," I said.

Danna helped me up. "Wrap the fabric around your wrists and ankles," she told me. I swung nearby Allie.

Then I saw Liam come into the gym. My big chance!

I quickly tried to flip.

But I flopped.

I tried to flip again. The fabric wrapped around my body.

"Marlo?" Liam's voice sounded muffled.

I tried to answer.

Mmmmpff. Fabric covered my mouth.

I was trapped inside a cocoon!

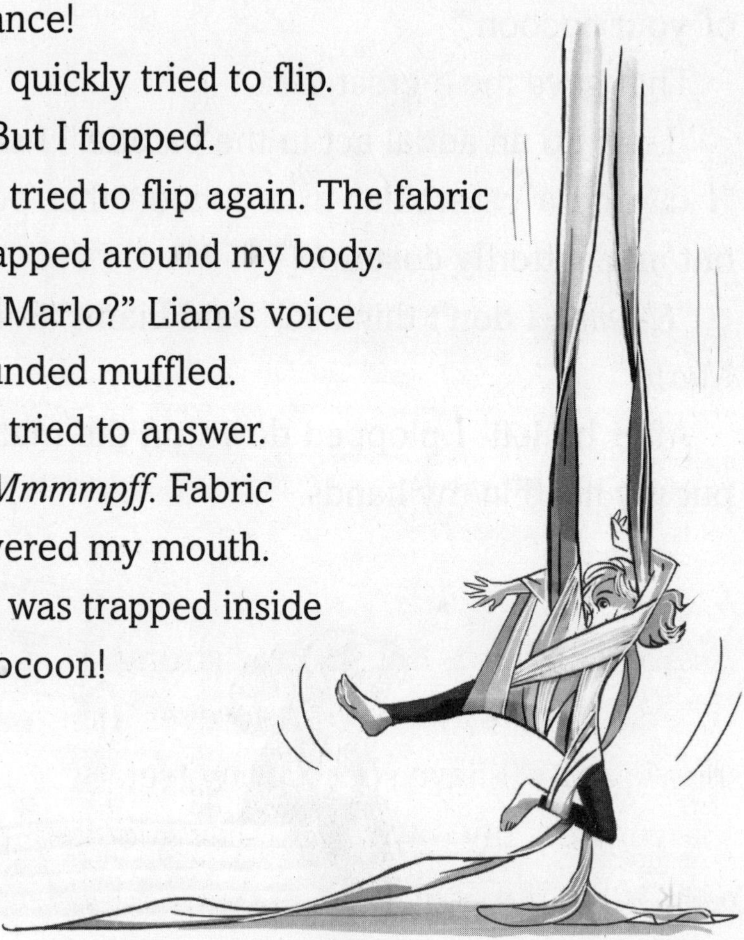

Liam and Allie unwrapped me.

"You're funny." Allie gave a friendly laugh.

"I'm funny when I'm *not* trying to be a clown!" I joked.

Liam chuckled. "My butterfly! You came out of your cocoon."

That gave me a great idea.

"I *can* do an aerial act in the parade!" I said. "I can be a caterpillar in a cocoon that pops out in a butterfly costume!"

"*Hmmm*. I don't think so," said Liam. "Sorry, Marlo."

After he left, I plopped down on the mats. I put my head in my hands.

"Hey," said Allie, sitting next to me. "The silks are really hard to learn. I'm not even that good at them yet."

I kept my head down.

"I'm sorry I was sort-of mean before," Allie blurted out.

I looked up. "Why don't you like me?"

"There have always been three Stardust Girls," Allie said. "I didn't want four. But you're funny and nice, and you try hard. I like you."

"So can we maybe be friends?" I asked.

“For sure!” said Allie.

“And I’m not giving up on the circus parade,” I added.

“You shouldn’t,” agreed Allie. “When I can’t do a trick on the trapeze, I keep at it. Or I try it another way.”

“Aerial arts take a lot of time to learn. What else can I try?” I asked.

“Well, Bella trains animals,” she said. “Do you like dogs?”

I’d never had a pet. But I’d always liked my friend Kira’s dog.

“I really like dogs,” I said, getting to my feet. “Let’s go find Bella!”

12 Downward Dog

Allie's family walked us back to the train. I spotted Bella and her white dogs out in a field with Carly.

"These flowers are all so pretty," Allie said, looking around.

"Let's pick some for the Pie Car," I said.

"Great idea! Let's pick *a lot*," Allie said.

She picked a big bunch. So did I.

Then we ran to Bella and Carly. I handed them each a flower.

A real one. No squirting flowers for me.

"Thanks," said Bella. Marshmallow, Coconut, and Tofu wagged their tails.

"I want to dance with animals in the circus parade—just like you!" I told Bella.

"I'll teach you!" Bella pushed the button on her music player. Happy music came out.

The three dogs circled Bella. She sang softly to them. Bella reached for Tofu's front paws. They danced.

"Your turn, Marlo," said Bella, stepping aside.

I put down my flowers. Then I boogied forward. I pretended that a crowd was cheering for me.

I waved the dogs over.

"Time to dance!" I shook my hips and my arms.

Tofu lay flat on the grass.

Coconut lay flat on the grass.

Marshmallow lay flat on the grass.

"Come on, doggies!" I danced some more.

The dogs did not boogie.

"Try using these." Bella handed me some dog treats.

"Yummy, yummy!" I showed the treats.

The dogs would not move.

"They love to jump through hoops," said Bella. She lifted up three hula-hoops from the grass. Then she made a clicking noise with her tongue.

Tofu jumped.

Coconut jumped.

Marshmallow jumped.

Bella handed me the hoops. I clicked my tongue, just like Bella had done.

All three dogs lay down. They would not jump.

"I stink at this—just like everything else." I slipped the hula-hoops over my head.

"No, you don't, Marlo. Maybe these dogs only understand Bella," said Allie.

"*All* animals understand Bella," added Carly. "That's her talent."

"Well, it is not mine." I blinked back my tears. I swayed my hips and got the hula-hoops spinning.

I moved my hips faster. The three hoops spun and spun.

The show was tomorrow. My two days were almost up.

"Oh, my!" cried Allie.

"Whoa!" said Bella.

"W-O-W. Wow!" said Carly.

They all stared at me.

"What?" I asked.

13 Add Sparkle

My three new friends stared at me with open mouths.

"You can hula-hoop?" asked Allie.

"She can hula-hoop!" said Bella.

My three hoops were still spinning.

"Sure," I said. "I've been hooping since I was little. It's no big deal."

"No big deal?" cried Carly. "It's fabulous!"

I shook my head. "It's playground stuff. Not circus stuff."

"Anything can be circus stuff," said Carly, "if you add sparkle and wow!"

"We need to show Liam," said Bella. "But he's busy in there." She pointed at the big tent.

"I have an idea. Keep hooping, Marlo." Allie pulled out her phone. She began to video me.

"Do something fabulous!" called Bella.

I hooped faster. I lifted one leg. I jumped and hooped. I spun and hooped.

Carly turned to Allie and Bella. "We need to get more hula-hoops."

"I have a lot." I told them about the hoops on my walls.

Carly ran to get them.

"We will help you make a hula-hoop dance," said Allie.

We worked on my dance until dinnertime. Soon I was spinning five hoops! I had no idea I could do that!

We skipped into the Pie Car. I put the wild flowers into glass jars. Then I put the jars on the tables with the new lavender tablecloths that Mrs. Bruni had sewed.

"Our makeover is working," said Bella.

"We should have a paint party," I said. "Let's paint these walls a happier color."

"Pink!" said Carly.

Somehow I knew she would say that. "Pink is awesome!" I said.

"What's awesome?" Liam asked, walking in.

"Marlo's new circus act is awesome," Bella said quickly.

"You *have* to see it," said Carly.

"Right now!" Allie handed her phone to Liam. Allie could be pushy sometimes. I was glad she was pushing for me now.

I held my breath. There I was on the screen. Hoops spinning on my hips. On my arms. On my legs.

The video stopped. Liam didn't say anything. We all waited.

My chest felt tight. I wanted *so much* for him to like it.

"You are one very determined girl, Marlo," Liam said. "You set your mind to something, and you don't stop until you do it."

I bit my lip. What did that mean?

"Your new act is fabulous, amazing, and awesome," he said. "You can be in tomorrow's parade."

I jumped up and down. "I'm a Stardust Girl?"

"No," Liam said suddenly.

I stopped jumping. We all stared at him.

"I changed the name." He grinned. "You all are now the *Amazing* Stardust Girls!"

Carly, Bella, Allie, and I cheered. We were ready to be amazing.

14 Bump a Nose

The next morning, I helped Mom frost a huge cake.

"I'm nervous about the show later," I said.

"Are you nervous-scared or nervous-excited?" Mom asked.

"I'm scared I'll mess up." I thought a moment. "But I'm excited, too."

"That's a good kind of nervous," she said.

I agreed.

"Hi, girls!" said Mom, as Allie, Carly, and Bella hurried in. "Looking for a snack?"

"Yes." Carly reached into a bowl for an apple. She was always hungry.

Allie swatted her hand. "Let's go get ready."

The four of us ran to the Dressing Room Car. I smiled the whole way there.

Inside, Carly handed me a sparkly rainbow-swirled unitard. "My mom sewed this for you. I know you like rainbows."

"It's so pretty!" I gasped.

"Hurry! Try it on." Allie pulled me behind a curtain.

I twirled in the rainbow costume. "What do you think?"

"More glitter." Carly swiped hot-pink glitter lipstick on my lips.

"More sparkle." Bella pressed rhinestones onto my cheeks.

"More shine." Allie pinned a gold crown of blinking lights to my hair.

Then I painted a rainbow on my face.

“Now you’re a Stardust Girl.” Allie put her arm around me.

“An *Amazing* Stardust Girl,” corrected Bella.

We all laughed.

“Bump a nose,” Carly said.

“What?” I said. I put both hands over my nose. “Why?”

“That’s what clowns say for good luck,” said Carly.

“Oh, I get it. Because clowns have big red noses,” I said.

“Not all clowns.” Carly had a pink star painted on the tip of *her* nose.

"Let's do it. It can be like our very own secret handshake. One . . . two . . . three . . . bump a nose!" called Allie.

We all bumped noses.

Owww!

"We should think of something else," Bella said, rubbing her nose.

A bell rang.

"That's the warning bell," said Carly.

"Time to get *our* costumes on," said Allie. "The circus is about to start!"

15 AMAZING!

I waited backstage. The parade wasn't until the very end of the show.

Mom stayed by my side. "Do you like the circus, Marlo?" she asked.

"Yes! I love it!" I cried.

Mom grinned. "I told you it would be a Great Adventure."

I gave her a big hug. "I can't wait to call Kira and tell her everything about our exciting new circus life."

“Marlo,” Carly said, tapping my arm. “It’s time! Let’s line up for the parade.”

We ran over to Bella and Allie. Tofu, Coconut, and Marshmallow were there, too.

The band played. Colorful lights swirled.

“Meet the Amazing Stardust Girls—Carly, Allie, and Bella!” called Liam.

Carly, Allie, and Bella skipped and flipped to the front of the parade line.

My heartbeat sounded even louder than the band’s big drums.

“And now for our newest Amazing Stardust Girl—Marlo!” Liam called.

I took a deep breath and walked into the bright spotlight. I couldn't see the crowd, but I heard them. Cheering. Stamping their feet.

I slipped all five hoops over my head. Each hoop was a different color. I began to circle my hips. Slowly, at first. Then faster and faster.

The hoops became a rainbow blur.
I lifted my arms and twirled.
The hoops kept spinning.
I skipped to the front of the parade.
The hoops kept spinning.

I had a fabulous talent all along. It just took me a little while to figure that out. And now the crowd was clapping for *me*.

Then I tossed my hoops to the side. Allie and Bella grabbed my hands. We did the parade dance. We kicked our legs high. Well, I kicked my legs kind-of-high.

We began to twirl.

Carly reached into the basket she carried.

She tossed sparkly pink glitter into the air!

Glitter landed on my hair and my cheeks. I sparkled all over.

I gave a happy twirl. I was an Amazing Stardust Girl in the big circus parade!

I didn't want the show to ever end.

But it did . . .

Back on the train, I wouldn't take off my rainbow costume. I loved it so much.

"You'll wear it again tomorrow," said Bella, "at the next show."

"And at the show after that," said Carly.

"And we'll do the parade *together*," Allie said. "Every time."

I couldn't wait! I hugged my new friends.

That night, I stared out my window. The sky was filled with twinkling stars. Everything at the Stardust Circus sparkled.

Even the sky.

HEATHER ALEXANDER lives in New Jersey, with her husband, two daughters, and a small white dog, who does very few tricks but is awfully cute.

When she was younger, Heather used to be a figure skater. She still loves everything to do with twirling, jumping, and glitter. Lots and lots of glitter!

Heather is the author of more than forty books for kids. THE AMAZING STARDUST FRIENDS is her first early chapter book series.

DIANE LE FEYER lives in a magical land called France, where there are lots of big castles and very good food. As a child, she was always drawing and dreaming of glitter and sparkle! As an adult, she makes her living drawing fantastical scenes, working in 2-D animation (both as a director and animator), and teaching young artists. She is a teacher, an artist, a bad cook, and a mother. She has a darling daughter, a loving husband, and a goldfish named Bubbles.

THE AMAZING STARDUST FRIENDS

STEP INTO THE SPOTLIGHT!

QUESTIONS & ACTIVITIES

Marlo loves the exciting adjectives Liam uses when he speaks, such as *amazing*, *fabulous*, and *awesome*. List more adjectives that have the **same** meaning.

What do the Stardust Girls wear when they perform? Look back at Chapter 1, and use the words and pictures to **describe** each costume.

Marlo is determined to find an act to perform in the circus parade. Discuss the acts she tries and whether or not she is successful.

Describe what school is like on the circus train. How is it **different from** and **similar to** your school?

What job would you do or what act would you perform if *you* lived on the Stardust Circus train?

scholastic.com/branches